Super Ways to
Jumpstart
the School Year!

by Michael Gravois

New York • Toronto • London • Auckland • Sydney
Mexico City • New Delhi • Hong Kong

SCHOLASTIC
PROFESSIONAL BOOKS

For the teachers in my family—
Stephen Hancock, Mae Gravois, Mary Ellen Gravois, Gayle Lund
Donna Tuerlings, Marsha Sykes, Rosemary Kerrin, Angelle Ruppert

Cover design by Norma Ortiz and Jaime Lucero
Interior design by Mindy Belter
Interior illustrations by Teresa Anderko

ISBN 0-439-05189-4
Copyright © 1999 by Michael Gravois. All rights reserved.

Printed in the U.S.A.

Contents

BulletinBoards
For the First Week of School . . . and Beyond

Getting Off to a Great Start!

Creating the Bulletin Board

Create a blue sky and a dark road as the background for your bulletin board. Add a title banner which says, "Getting Off to a Great Start in (Class Name)." Curve the title banner outward a few times to give it a three-dimensional effect.

On the first day of school give each student a copy of the runner template on page 9. Ask students to draw on hair to reflect their own hairstyle and color and to write their name in large, creative letters on the flag that the runner is holding. After they finish coloring the runner, they should cut the figure out and give it to you. Staple the runners onto the bulletin board. Curve the flags outward a couple of times so it looks like they're blowing in the breeze.

If you have time, you could first have the students create background art—houses, clouds, trees, and so on—before you staple up the runners.

Birthday Blowout

Creating the Bulletin Board

Use the template on page 9 to post the birthdays of all of the members of your class.

- ■ Write the month on the cake platter.
- ■ On the cake itself, list the names of students who have birthdays that falls within that month.
- ■ Color the cakes and hang them across the wall of the classroom.

You might want to color the cakes first, laminate them, and then write the names in washable marker, so you can use the cakes in future years.

Flower Power

Creating the Bulletin Board

Use two colors of bulletin board paper for the background so that the pots look like they're sitting on a shelf.

Making the Pots

You should create the flower pots before the first day of school. First, make as many copies of the flower pot template on page 10 as you have class jobs, and then follow these instructions to construct them:

1. Glue the template page onto a sheet of construction paper.
2. Cut out the pot and the pot's bottom.
3. On the construction paper side of the pot, use a marker to draw a horizontal line an inch from the top of the pot to create a lip (similar to the one on the template side).
4. Write the title of the class job across the front of the pot using a large marker or dimensional paint.
5. If you'd like, you can now laminate the pot for extra durability. (If you do laminate, use dimensional paint after laminating.)
6. Tape tab #1 onto the dot in the lower left corner of the pot.
7. Tape tabs #2-5 along the bottom edge of the pot while curving the pot so that it arches outward.
8. Bend tab #6 upward and tape it to the bulletin board.
9. Lift the pot and tape tabs #7-10 so that they are hidden within the pot.

Attach them to your bulletin board either in a straight line (as shown above) or in a random pattern on a more vertical bulletin board.

Making the Flowers

During the first day of school give each student a copy of the flower template on page 11.

■ First, have students write their name in large bold letters within the center of the two flowers.
■ Next, have them color the flowers as they desire.
■ Then, they should cut the flowers out and glue them back to back around the top of a plastic drinking straw.
■ Finally, they should color the leaves green, wrap each of them around the middle of the drinking straw, and glue them in place.

Put the flowers in a large pot labeled "PICK ME!". Choose students to perform each of the jobs by placing their flower in the corresponding job pot. Change students each week. Use the class list template on page 35 to keep track of which students have performed each job.

Welcome to School

■ Creating the Bulletin Board

If not handled quickly and efficiently, taking attendance and lunch count can waste time and cause students to lose focus. This bulletin board allows you to do both with minimal student involvement, allowing them to remain focused on a morning activity.

On the first day of school give each of your students a copy of the fish template on page 12. First, they color in a fish and glue it onto a sheet of oaktag for durability. Then they should cut the fish out, write their name across the fish's side, and color it. Collect the fish and laminate them so they can be used throughout the year.

You will need to have already set up the background for this bulletin board before the start of school. It should be located near the door where students enter in the morning. Begin by covering the area with green paper so it looks like grass. Using blue bulletin board paper, create a large pond at the top of the bulletin board. Add the "Welcome to School" sign on page 55 to this pond. Create two smaller ponds and place them at the bottom; create two signs (using the blank sign template on page 12) to place on these ponds, as shown in the illustration. You may want to create different titles depending on the lunch choices your students need to make, such as "Bag Lunch" and "Cafeteria Lunch." If you have the time to be really creative, you might want to make some cattails out of construction paper to place around the ponds and add other background details. Curl some of the grass fronds to make them three dimensional. Finally, add one half of a Velcro dot onto the back of each fish, and put the matching half in the large pond. Put two strips of Velcro across the two smaller ponds. Double-back Velcro tape can be purchased at most office supply stores.

When the students arrive each morning the fish should be in the large pond. As they walk into the room they should remove their fish and place them in the smaller pond which corresponds to their lunch choice. The names that remain in the large pond reflect absent students. Count the fish in the lower ponds to take lunch count. These tasks can be completed while the students are starting their work in the morning. When the students return from lunch they should move their fish back to the large pond to be ready for the next day. Any fish that remain in the lower ponds reflect students who did not return from lunch.

In the News

Class Discussions

Reporting on the news of the day is a sure way to generate great class discussions. Each day have a different student bring in an article of his or her choice and present the information to the class. You can use the Class List Template on page 35 to keep track of which students have presented their articles. The student should fill out the information sheet on page 13 to help organize his or her thoughts.

Creating the Bulletin Board

Divide your bulletin board into four quadrants. Use different colors of bulletin board paper to define each area. Copy and color the newsboy on page 14 and place him in the center of the bulletin board. Label each quadrant according to the locale of the news (i.e., City, State, Country, and World) or by type of news (Politics, Sports, Entertainment, Events, etc.). After students makes their presentations, open the floor up for questions and meaningful discussion. Place the article in the appropriate section, replacing the last article that was there.

Student Accountability

It is hard for many students to stand in front of a group of their peers and give an oral presentation. Regular exposure to oral speaking will help them overcome their fears as they continually meet with success. Holding students accountable for talking loudly and maintaining eye contact with the audience during the presentation forces them to confront their fears and improve their public speaking skills. Use the evaluation guide at the bottom of the form on page 13 to give each student a grade based on the presentation. You can use this as a homework or class participation grade.

Keys to Success

Creating the Bulletin Board

Words of wisdom make people think about many facets of the life experience. I like to create a bulletin board where you can spotlight a different quote each week. Every Monday morning begin the week by reading the quote and discussing its meaning.

Copy the key template on page 14. Glue them to yellow construction paper before you cut them out. Cover them with gold glitter so they sparkle. Add a banner entitled "Keys to Success." Write thought-provoking quotes on chart paper and hang them under the title.

Keep the quotes organized by punching two holes in the top of the chart paper and using a ring clip to keep them together. Throughout the years as you accumulate quotes you might consider having a quote of the day.

Finding Quotes

There are many places where you can find meaningful words of wisdom. The Readers' Digest has a page called "Quotable Quotes" in each issue, and there are desk calendars which have a quote a day. Quotes can also be found in books and magazines. Once you begin collecting them, they'll turn up regularly. Encourage students to find some, too. Here are some of my favorites:

"It is never too late to be what you might have been." *George Eliot*

"Take sides. Neutrality helps the oppressor, never the victim. Silence encourages the tormentor, never the tormented." *Elie Weisel*

"Genius is one percent inspiration and ninety-nine percent perspiration." *Thomas Edison*

"The dictionary is the only place where success comes before work." *Vince Lombardi*

"Failing to plan is a plan to fail." *Effie Jones*

"Stand up for what is right, even if you're standing alone."

"History . . . learning about what was can help you turn what is into what will be."

"Today is the day you make your choices for tomorrow."

"Judgment comes from experience and great judgment comes from bad experience."

"What is popular is not always right. What is right is not always popular."

"Education is your passport to the future, for tomorrow belongs to those who prepare for it today." *Malcolm X*

"The best way to defeat your enemy is to make him your friend."

"You are not finished when you lose. You are finished when you quit.

"Whether you think you can or think you can't—you are right." *Henry Ford*

Runner Template

- Add a face and hair to the figure below so that it looks like you.
- Write your name across the banner in large, creative lettering.
- Color the runner and cut it out.
- Have your teacher staple the runner onto the bulletin board.

← *Place on fold*

- You may want to enlarge these templates on your copier.

Cake Template

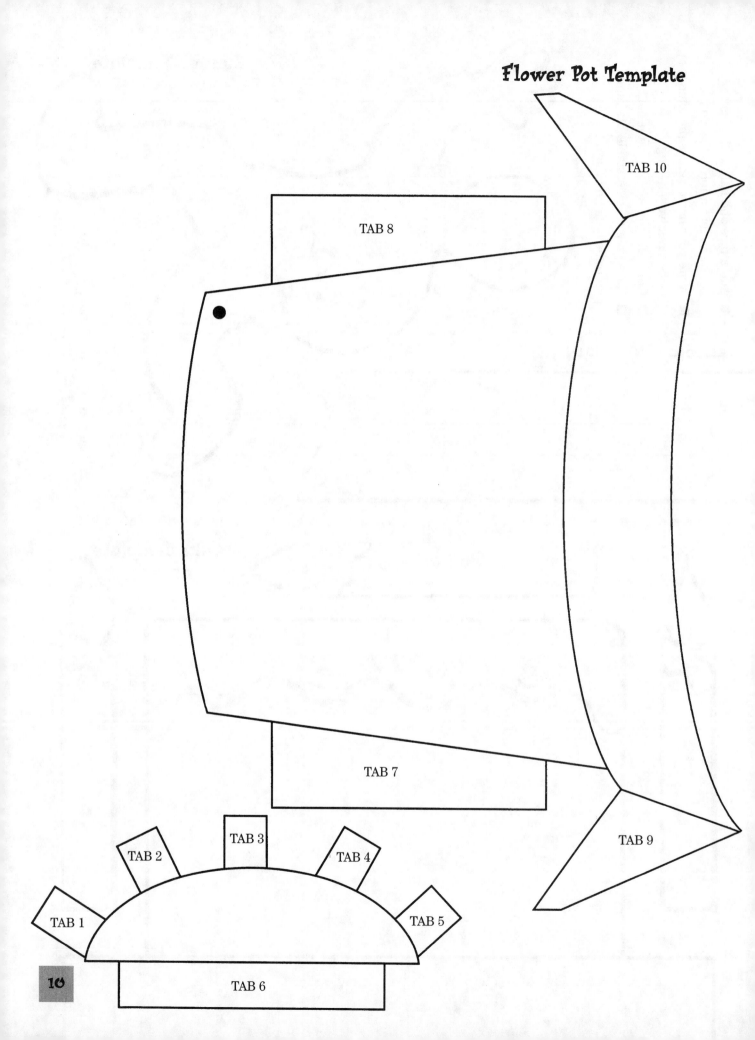

Flower Pot Template

TAB 10

TAB 8

TAB 7

TAB 9

TAB 1

TAB 2

TAB 3

TAB 4

TAB 5

TAB 6

10

Flower Template

- Write your name in the center of the two flowers.
- Color the flowers in your favorite colors.
- Cut out the flowers and glue them back to back around a drinking straw.
- Color the leaves green and wrap them around the straw, gluing them back to back.
- Put your flower in the PICK ME pot.

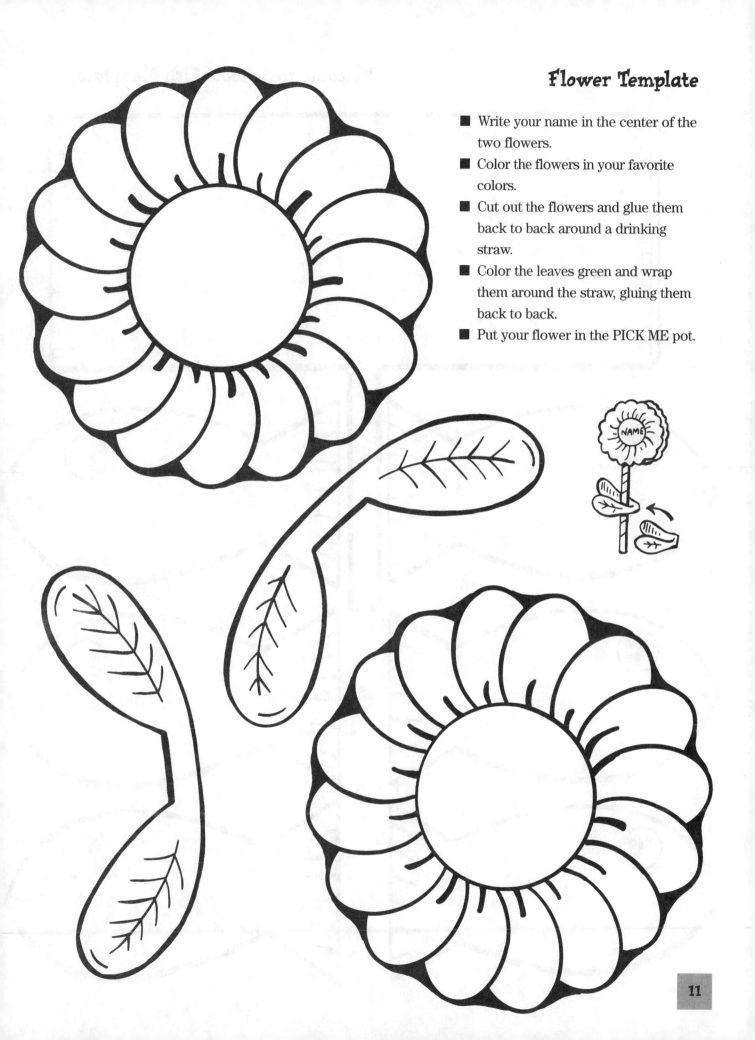

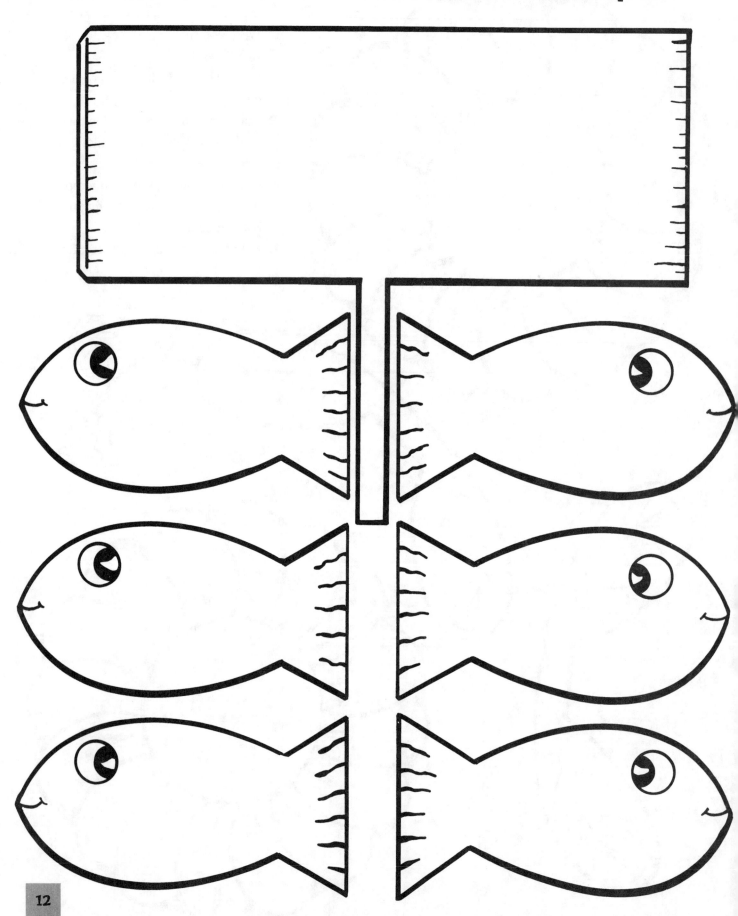

In The News

A good newspaper article always includes the 5 W's. When discussing your news article, be sure to include the following:

■ Article Headline: _____

■ **W**ho is the article about? _____

■ **W**hat is the article about? _____

_____

_____

■ **W**here does it take place? _____

■ **W**hen does it take place? _____

■ **W**hy did you choose this article? (Do not just say, "Because it was interesting."):

_____

_____

_____

_____

_____

_____

For Teacher's Use: Do Not Write Below This Line

....

Score____

	Consistently									Never
The article was brought in on time.	10	9	8	7	6	5	4	3	2	1
The information above was filled out completely.	10	9	8	7	6	5	4	3	2	1
The student spoke knowledgeably about the article.	10	9	8	7	6	5	4	3	2	1
The student spoke loudly and clearly.	10	9	8	7	6	5	4	3	2	1
The student maintained eye contact with the audience.	10	9	8	7	6	5	4	3	2	1

Key Template

Activities

For the First Week of School ... and Beyond

Find Someone Who ...

This game is a wonderful ice breaker for the first day of school. It's like a socially interactive scavenger hunt which allows students to get to know each other. You'll be amazed by the buzz of excitement that this activity generates and by the interesting conversations which take place when reviewing the winner's category sheet.

- Copy the "Find Someone Who…" form on page 19.
- Give students fifteen minutes to find classmates who fit the listed categories, without listing the same person for more than two categories. When fifteen minutes are up, have the students add up the total number of categories they completed and write the total at the top of the page.
- Ask everyone to stand. Then start counting up to 25. Students should sit when you say the number which matches their total. The last standing student is the winner.
- Take the winner's sheet and review it with the class. Talk to each of the students whose name is listed under each category. Verify that they fit the given category. If they do not, deduct one point from the total. Continue until the winner is established.
- Decide on some small prize for the winner to receive, such as a book, a free computer pass, lunch with the teacher, etc.

Interest Inventory

It is important that you get to know your students as unique individuals. The responses they give on the interest inventory on pages 20-21 provide an insight into how they view the world, as well as what they find fun and exciting. This may help you choose class novels and activities throughout the year.

- Copy the "Interest Inventory" forms on pages 20-21 back to back.
- Assign it for homework during the first week of school.
- Review the inventories and note any patterns you see which might help you plan future activities.
- Save the inventories and return them at the end of the year so the students can see how their attitudes, likes, and dislikes have changed.

The next three activities are end-of-the-year activities in which students make things to be shared with the class you'll have the following year. If this is your first year teaching, your students will still enjoy reading *The Teacher From the Black Lagoon* (see Survival Guides below).

Survival Guides

All teachers have quirks which either endear them to their students or which make students squirm. This activity will help students understand some of the things that will be expected of them during the coming year as well as give them an idea of teacher quirks that they should "watch out for."

Before beginning this activity, call students together in the reading area—a large rug works well—and read them the picture book, *The Teacher From the Black Lagoon* by Mike Thaler (published by Scholastic). This story helps them understand that many of the fears they have about their new teacher are unfounded.

Then pass out the "Survival Guides" which were made during the last days of school by your former class. Those students will have created little books which detail things that the next year's class needs to "watch out for." Here's what your class should do at the end of the year:

- Each student should create a little book following the instructions on page 22.
- On the cover, students should write a title which includes their names, such as "Rebeccah's Survival Guide to Mr. Gravois's Class."
- On each of the pages, including the backcover, they should write a sentence which describes something to watch out for throughout the year, such as "Beware when Mr. Gravois gives you the evil eye!" or "Beware of talking during fire drills—you'll get a warning!" They should draw a picture to accompany each survival tip.

ABC's of Our Class

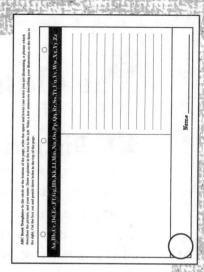

ABC books make a fun culminating activity for the end of the year. They provide a means for students to reflect on the things they learned throughout the year, the activities they participated in, and the field trips they went on. They're also a great introduction to the year ahead if you read them to your new class on the first day of school.

- Write the letters A-Z down the left side of a large piece of chart paper.
- As a class brainstorm all the things that the students learned and did throughout the year that begin with each letter.
- Choose one item from each letter that best reflects the year.
- Pass out a copy of the template on page 23 to each student.
- Each student will select a different letter and do the following:
  - illustrate the idea in the left-hand box,
  - write the upper and lower case letter and a word or phrase (beginning with that letter) which explains the picture in the left-hand box,
  - write a few sentences in the right-hand box which describes the topic,
  - write his or her name at the bottom of the page.
- Collect the pages and alphabetize them. Create a cover which says "The ABC's of XXX Class". (Fill in the grade you teach.) Bind the pages together.
- On the first day of the next school year read the "ABC's of XXX Class" to your new class. This gets them excited about all the things they will do in the coming year.

A Lockbook to the Person Who Sits in My Desk

This activity allows each student to "connect" with someone from the year before. At the end of each year, have your students create a lockbook which will be given to the person who sits in his/her desk on the first day of the next school year. Copy the templates on pages 25-26 back to back so that the cover panel is opposite panel two. The lockbook describes fun things the class did throughout the year, and it explains why the new student needn't be nervous about the year ahead. Instructions for constructing a lockbook can be found on page 24.

The Classroom Community

Discussing the Classroom Community

This is a great activity for the first day of school which should take place while you are discussing your class rules. First, have a large grid pre-drawn on a sheet of bulletin board or chart paper which has the word "COMMUNITY" written in large letters in the center of the grid. Hang it on the blackboard at the front of the class. Then tell your students that "community" is defined as a body of people living in the same place under the same laws, and ask them to explain how their classroom fits this definition. Ask them how they would define a successful community, leading them to conclude that the same ideas would apply to having a successful classroom. They should realize that the class must work together as a group to ensure a happy, productive environment for the coming year. Encourage them to understand that even though a class is thought of as a group of people, all groups are made up of individuals, and each individual is responsible for being a contributing member of the community.

Ask students to name members of the community at large (leaders, workers, all kinds of people). List them on the board. Then ask students who some of the members of the school community are. Add the most important names (the principal, the secretary, the nurse, and so on) to the grid, interlocking the letters crossword style. Then add your name to the list as the leader of the classroom community. Randomly select students to approach the grid to add their names to the community. When all of the students have added their names, begin discussing the rules that the classroom will need to adopt in order to ensure a successful school year.

				Z														
			C	O	M	M	U	N	I	T	Y						
			E		S.												
					B												
					R												
			N	O	E	L	L	E									
				O		I											
			K	Y	L	E											
			S		Y												

Find Someone Who . . .

Find someone in the class who fits each of the following categories. Record their name. You cannot use the same person more than twice. Circle the number of each category you've completed.

1. Can name the 5 Great Lakes. NAME:_____

   (List them.) _____

   _____

2. Loves to read. NAME: _____

   (What kind of books?) _____

3. Has a younger brother. NAME: _____

   (Brother's name?) _____

4. Has two older sisters. NAME: _____

   (Sisters' names?) _____

5. Enjoys gardening. NAME: _____

6. Has tried asparagus. NAME: _____

7. Can speak several words of a foreign language.

   NAME:_____ (What language?)_____

8. Has brown eyes. NAME: _____

9. Likes to use the computer. NAME:_____

10. Can play a musical instrument. NAME:_____

    (What instrument?)_____

11. Has a birthday in November. NAME: _____

    (What date?) _____

12. Plays on a sports team. NAME: _____

    (What sport?_____What's the team's name?)

    _____

13. Owns a collection of items. NAME: _____

    (What is it?) _____

14. Owns more than three pets. NAME: _____

    (What are they?) _____

    _____

15. Has performed in a play before. NAME: _____

    (What was the name of the play?) _____

    _____

16. Likes to write stories. NAME: _____

17. Has lived in another state. NAME: _____

    (Which state?) _____

18. Has seen a chicken hatch before._____

    NAME:_____(When?) _____

19. Knows what a thesaurus is. NAME: _____

    (What is it?) _____

    _____

20. Has made dinner for the family. NAME: _____

    (What did they make?)_____

    _____

21. Loves to draw. NAME: _____

22. Knows the name of the Vice President.

    NAME: _____

    (What is it?) _____

23. Knows the name of the governor.

    NAME: _____

    (What is it?) _____

24. Knows the capital of Vermont.

    NAME: _____

    (What is it?) _____

25. Knows the chemical formula for water.

    NAME: _____

    (What is it?) _____

Interest Inventory

1. If you could be *anything* in the world when you grow up, what would you be? Why? (Realistic answers only. Not "a horse" or "a time traveler.") _____

2. What are your hobbies? _____

3. If you could travel any place in the world, where would you go? _____

4. To what clubs do you belong? _____

5. What club activity do you like best? _____

6. Do you take any special lessons outside of school? What? (Music, sports, dance, acting, singing, etc.) _____

7. What kinds of activities do you like to do with friends? _____

8. What kinds of activities do you like to do all by yourself? _____

9. What is your favorite sport? _____

10. What is your favorite TV show? Why _____

    _____

11. What is your favorite movie of all time? _____

12. What is your favorite animal? _____

13. If you could be like any one great person, whom would you choose? _____

14. What do you do at home when you have time to do anything you wish? _____

    _____

15. Set a goal for yourself regarding school in the coming year. Be specific. (Not "I want better grades.") _____

16. If you were given $1,000, what would you do with it? _____

17. Check the subjects you like to do the most in school:

    ❑ Art   ❑ Math   ❑ Reading   ❑ Writing   ❑ Computers

    ❑ P.E.   ❑ Science   ❑ Music   ❑ Social Studies   ❑ Spelling

18. When did you last read a book? What was the title? _____

19. What is your favorite book of all time? _____

20. What magazines do you like to read? _____

21. What parts of the newspaper do you like to read? _____

22. Put a check in the box that tells how much you like each of the following types of stories:

	One of My Favorite Kinds	A Lot	Somewhat	Not Too Much	Not At All
Animal Stories					
Fantasy & Myth					
Space					
Science					
Adventure					
Sports					
Westerns					
History					
Real People (Biographies)					
Romance					
Science Fiction					
Horror					
Poetry					
Short Stories					
Mysteries					
Comic Books					
Magazines					
Newspapers					
Picture Books					

Creating a Little Book

1. Fold a sheet of paper in half widthwise.

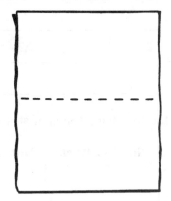

2. Fold it in half again in the same direction.

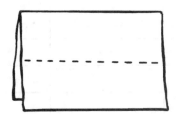

3. Fold this long narrow strip in half in the opposite direction.

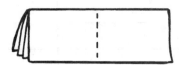

4. Open the paper up to the Step 2 position, and cut halfway down the vertical fold.

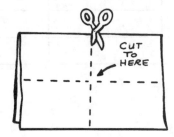

5. Open the paper up and turn it horizontally. There should be a hole in the center of the paper where you'd made the cut.

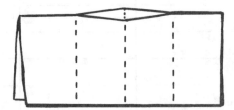

6. Fold the paper in half lengthwise.

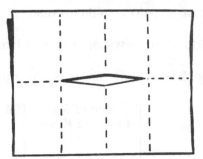

7. Push in on the ends of the paper so the slit opens up. Push until the center panels meet.

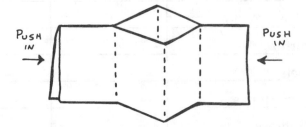

8. Fold the four pages into a book and crease the edges.

ABC Book Template: In the circle at the bottom of the page, write the upper and lower case letter you are illustrating. Draw your illustration in the box on the left. Write a few sentences describing your illustration on the lines to the right. Add your name and a short title. Cut the box out and punch three holes in the top of the page.

Aa,Bb,Cc,Dd,Ee,Ff,Gg,Hh,Ii,Jj,Kk,Ll,Mm,Nn,Oo,Pp,Qq,Rr,Ss,Tt,Uu,Vv,Ww,Xx,Yy,Zz

Name

Title

Creating a Lock Book

These instructions are based on using half pages. However, any size page can be used. It need not be cut in half first. Experiment using different sizes.

1. Cut the page in half widthwise.

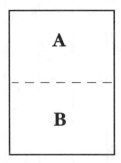

2. Fold both sheets in half widthwise.

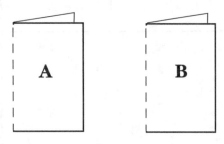

3. Open the pages and measure along the crease, placing three small pencil marks at the 1/4 point, the 1/2 point, and the 3/4 point.

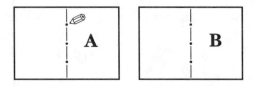

4. Cut the center of one crease from the 1/4 point to the 3/4 point. (It may be helpful to first fold the paper in half lengthwise, but be careful not to crease it.)

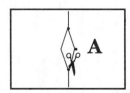

5. Cut the other page along the crease twice, both times from the edge of the paper in to the 1/4 points.

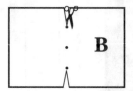

6. Curl one side of the page that was cut twice, and feed it through the hole in the other paper. Open it up so it locks into place.

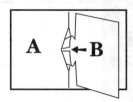

7. Fold it into a book shape. (Make sure the pages are in the correct order if you're using a template.)

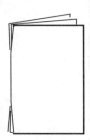

8. Additional twice-cut pages can be fed through the page with the hole in the center to increase the book's length.

Calm Down!

I know you're nervous because it's the first day of school, but here's why you shouldn't be anxious about the year ahead.

_____

_____

_____

_____

_____

_____

_____

_____

_____

A Lockbook
to the Person Who Sits in My Desk

Constructing a Lock Book

1. Cut the page in half along the dotted line.

2. Cut along the other dashed lines.

3. Feed the other page through the hole in this page. Make sure page three follows page two. Open it up so it locks into place.

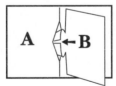

4. Fold into a book shape.

5. Draw a self-portrait on the front cover. Be creative. Write your name below it.

Top 10 List

The ten favorite things I did in school this year:

#10 _____

#9 _____

#8 _____

#7 _____

#6 _____

#5 _____

#4 _____

#3 _____

#2 _____

And the #1 favorite thing I did was . . .

Getting to Know Me

Here's a paragraph about me and my interests.

_____

_____

_____

_____

_____

_____

_____

_____

Read All About It!

Let me tell you about the favorite thing we did this year—what I did, what I learned, and how I felt.

_____

_____

_____

_____

_____

_____

_____

_____

The #1 Favorite Thing I Did in School This Year!

My Teacher

Here's a picture of my teacher and a sentence describing something I liked about her/him.

_____

_____

Classroom Management
For the First Week of School . . . and Beyond

Establishing Class Rules

Sit down with your class on the first day of school and discuss the importance that rules play in the daily lives of any large group of people. Without certain rules there would be chaos, hurt feelings, and little accomplished. Students do understand the importance of rules and, when asked, can tell you the rules that contribute to an orderly, well-managed classroom. Ask the students what rules they have had in past classrooms and why those rules were important. Write the suggested rules on the blackboard. After all of the rules are discussed, select (with the students' input) the four or five most important rules. Phrase them in a positive way and write them on chart paper. At the bottom of the chart paper write, "I understand our class rules" and have each student sign the document. Hang it on the wall for all to see throughout the year.

Class Rules
1. Always speak your mind— just use your hand first.
2. Never hurt another living thing— on the inside or the outside.
3. Listen when others are speaking.
4. Move slowly in classrooms and hallways.
5. Respect others and their property.

I understand our class rules.

Darcy Dara Woody Peter Jessica
Jake Zack Kathleen Lily Brianna
Caitlin Brooks Joshua

Rewards and Consequences

REWARDS
for Obeying Rules

Praise from teacher
Points for team
Good Report Card
Raffle tickets
Homework Latepass
Happy phone call to parents

CONSE
for Disob

1st W
Name

2nd W
Name recorded plus ✓

3rd Warning
• 2 Paragraph apology
• Parents called
• 15 minutes before school

It is important for you to let your students know what your expectations are, what the rewards will be if they follow the rules, and what the consequences will be if they disobey the rules. Develop a clear set of guidelines, review them with the class, post them near your class rules, and adhere to them consistently. Following through with the consequences lets the students know that infractions will not be tolerated. Rewarding students for observing the rules lets them know that good behavior is noticed and appreciated. Believe me, word spreads throughout the classroom when you call a student's parents in order to praise the child; such a phone call is also appreciated by the parents.

After the second infraction, I have my students write a two-paragraph apology describing what they did wrong, why that action cannot be allowed, and what they will do differently in the future. The apology must be signed by a parent. This assures me that the parents know about the problem on the day that it occurs.

While You Were Out

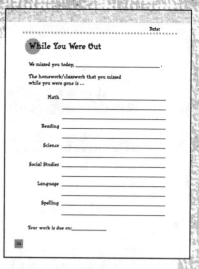

Student absences can become an added burden to the workload a teacher faces. The teacher needs to make sure the absent students know what happened on the day they missed and what work they need to make up. These forms offer a solution to that problem.

- Make two dozen copies of the "While You Were Out" form on page 32.
- Tape the sides of a manila folder so it forms a pocket, and staple the pocket folder to a bulletin board.
- Place the "While You Were Out" forms in the folder for easy access.
- Whenever a student is absent, place one of the forms on his desk along with a manila folder.
- The student sitting next to the absent child is responsible for filling out the form after each class, listing what the class did that day, what pages were read, and what the homework assignments are. The student should also insert any worksheets into the folder.
- When the absent student returns to school all of the missed classwork and homework is clearly listed. Or, if a sibling or parent stops by on the day of the absence, you need only hand them the folder and any textbooks that are needed.

Clock Partners

Teachers often need a way of randomly pairing students. Having students work as "clock partners" provides you with a way to do this quickly and easily.

- Pass out a copy of the "clock partners" template on page 33.
- Have students glue the template to a piece of oaktag to make it more durable and then cut it out.
- They should write their own names within the central circle.
- Tell students to find a classmate. Have them write their names within the one o'clock wedge on their partner's template.
- Tell them to find another partner. Have them write their names within the two o'clock wedge.
- Have them continue until they fill up each wedge through eleven o'clock. Have them leave the twelve o'clock space blank so you can fill it in. This allows you to pair up students based on ability or other criteria.

- Set certain guidelines before starting this activity, such as—
  - You must have the same number of boys as girls on your wheel.
  - Do not turn anyone away who approaches you, unless you have the required number of names.
- Collect the wheels and fill in the twelve o'clock partners.
- Laminate them if you have access to a machine.
- Return the wheels and have students keep them in an accessible place (in a binder or folder, or in their desk).
- Whenever you need to randomly pair students call out, for example, "Everybody find their four o'clock partners!" The students will check their wheels and pair up with their four o'clock partners.

Nameplates

Students can make nameplates on the first day of school so you and other students can easily learn everyone's name. (Use the template on page 33.) Collect the nameplates after a week and hold on to them so they can be used throughout the year when a substitute comes into your classroom.

Homework Assignment Sheets

Students can use the template on page 34 to record homework assignments. These can be kept in their binder or folder throughout the week.

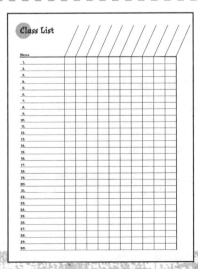

Class Lists

Write the names of your students on the class list template on page 35. Make copies and use them throughout the year for checking homework, keeping records of students who brought in their field trip money and permission slips, marking test grades, or "checking" students for misbehavior. Carry this template around on a clipboard for easy access.

Calendar Template

Students can use the calendar template on page 36 to keep track of long-term assignments. Use "mini" due dates to make long-term assignments more manageable. For recurring assignments, such as the "Classroom Chronicle" (see page 13) or "In The News" (see page 47), you can use the template to record students' names under the date that they are to turn in their work.

Appointment Wheels

Glue the appointment wheel template on page 37 to a heavy piece of cardboard. Use an exact-o knife to cut it out. Write each student's name on a wooden clothespin and hang the clothespins on a string which spans a bulletin board or wall. When students are in the middle of a writing assignment and need to conference with you, they should take their clothespin off the line and fasten it to the next available appointment slot on the appointment wheel. The wheel can sit near the conference area for easy reference. Call up each student sequentially. This prevents continual interruptions while speaking with individual students. After each mini-conference have students hang their clothespins back on the line.

Cooperative Grouping

Use cooperative grouping as a classroom management tool! Whenever my class begins a new social studies or science topic I divide my class up into groups of four or five students. Members of each group push their desks together into prearranged "islands." I allow some socialization time by having each island pick a group name, based on something shared by each group member—i.e., all members have names that contain only five letters ("The Quintuplets"), all members own a cat ("The Feline Fanciers"), all members are wearing red that day ("The Red Barons"). Students get to know interesting things about each other as they decide upon a name. Each group then designs a poster which contains its name and a logo. I hang the signs above each group from the lighting fixtures.

I hang a laminated chart, like the one illustrated below, near my desk where I write each group name. The groups can earn cooperative group points. I write the names and points with an erasable marker so the chart can be used throughout the year. Each group that earns a predetermined number of points by the end of the unit wins a "Homework Late Pass" (see page 41) for each member. Since each group has the opportunity to win, it eliminates the competitive aspect of the contest, as each group is only competing against itself. Points can be earned in various ways, and I try to allow each team to succeed—although sometimes a team does not. I will make announcements like—"Ten points to each team that quietly puts its things away and has its social studies books opened to page 76 within two minutes," "Twenty points to each team whose members are absolutely quiet during the fire drill," "Fifteen points to each team that works as a group to correctly answer nine of the ten questions on page 30." Awarding points not only excites the teams because of the "contest" element, but it makes each team member feel accountable for following the directions since individual performance could affect the team's score.

Cooperative Group Points

GROUP NAME	GOAL: 250 points					BY: December 21st							TOTAL
GROUP 1 The Band Members	25	15	10	20	10	15	20						
GROUP 2 The Mightly R's	25	15	10	20	15	20							
GROUP 3 The Travelers	25	10	20	10	15								
GROUP 4 The Gym Socks	25	15	10	20	10	15	20						
GROUP 5 The Mellow Yellows	25	15	20	15	15	20							

While You Were Out

We missed you today, _____ .

The homework/classwork that you missed
while you were gone is ...

Math _____

_____

Reading _____

_____

Science _____

_____

Social Studies _____

_____

Language Arts _____

_____

Spelling _____

_____

Your work is due on:_____

Clock Partners

- Write your name in the center of the wheel.
- Glue this sheet onto a piece of oaktag and then cut the wheel out.
- Listen to your teacher to find out how to fill up the clock partners template.

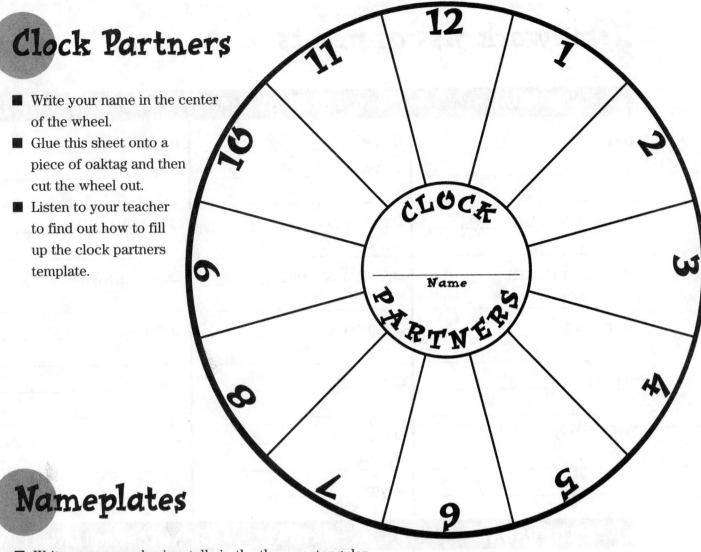

Nameplates

- Write your name horizontally in the three rectangular boxes. Use creative lettering.
- Cut out the figure along the dashed lines and fold it along the solid lines.
- Glue the long tab behind the panel it meets.
- Set the nameplate on your desk so it can easily be seen.

Homework Assignments

MONDAY

DATE: _____

❑ MATH: _____
_____

❑ LANGUAGE ARTS: _____
_____

❑ SOCIAL STUDIES: _____
_____

❑ SCIENCE: _____
_____

❑ READING: _____
_____

❑ SPELLING: _____
_____
_____

TUESDAY

DATE: _____

❑ MATH: _____
_____

❑ LANGUAGE ARTS: _____
_____

❑ SOCIAL STUDIES: _____
_____

❑ SCIENCE: _____
_____

❑ READING: _____
_____

❑ SPELLING: _____
_____

WEDNESDAY

DATE: _____

❑ MATH: _____
_____

❑ LANGUAGE ARTS: _____
_____

❑ SOCIAL STUDIES: _____
_____

❑ SCIENCE: _____
_____

❑ READING: _____
_____

❑ SPELLING: _____
_____

THURSDAY

DATE: _____

❑ MATH: _____
_____

❑ LANGUAGE ARTS: _____
_____

❑ SOCIAL STUDIES: _____
_____

❑ SCIENCE: _____
_____

❑ READING: _____
_____

❑ SPELLING: _____
_____

FRIDAY

DATE: _____

❑ MATH: _____
_____

❑ LANGUAGE ARTS: _____
_____

❑ SOCIAL STUDIES: _____
_____

❑ SCIENCE: _____
_____

❑ READING: _____
_____

❑ SPELLING: _____
_____

NOTES and LONG-TERM ASSIGNMENTS

_____
_____
_____
_____
_____
_____
_____
_____
_____
_____
_____
_____
_____
_____

Class List

Name										
1.										
2.										
3.										
4.										
5.										
6.										
7.										
8.										
9.										
10.										
11.										
12.										
13.										
14.										
15.										
16.										
17.										
18.										
19.										
20.										
21.										
22.										
23.										
24.										
25.										
26.										
27.										
28.										
29.										
30.										

SUNDAY	MONDAY	TUESDAY	WEDNESDAY	THURSDAY	FRIDAY	SATURDAY
☐	☐	☐	☐	☐	☐	☐
☐	☐	☐	☐	☐	☐	☐
☐	☐	☐	☐	☐	☐	☐
☐	☐	☐	☐	☐	☐	☐
☐	☐	☐	☐	☐	☐	☐

Appointment Wheel

■ Glue this sheet onto a heavy piece of cardboard and then cut the wheel out with an art knife.

■ Students can attach their clothespins to the appointment wheel when they need to ask you a question or hold a mini-conference during writing assignments.

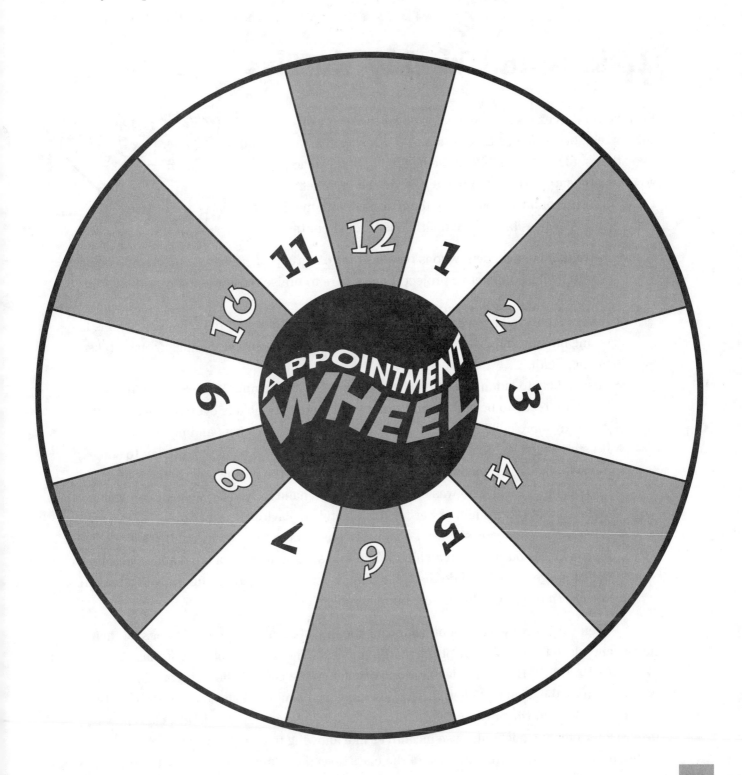

Motivational Strategies
for the First Week of School . . . and Beyond

Tickets and Weekly Raffles

Positive reinforcement not only helps boost the receiving child's self-esteem, but it also calls attention to a behavior that you would like other students to exhibit. At the beginning of the school year I go to a party supply store and buy a generic roll of tickets. Every day I tear off a strip of tickets and carry them around with me. I find as many reasons as possible to give out tickets throughout the day—

- I give them to a student who is on a task or to a group of students who are diligently working on a cooperative project. I make sure to praise the students by saying, "You sure are working hard!"

- If a student is talking while I'm giving a whole-group lesson, I find someone who is listening intently and give him a ticket while saying, "You sure are doing a great job listening, Keith."

- I use tickets to aid in transitions between subjects by saying, "I see Stephanie and Wade are ready to begin." When those two students get tickets everyone else tries to get ready more quickly. I might even then give out more tickets and praise.

- If I start to have problems with students calling out, I will hand out a ticket to someone with his or her hand raised and say, "Thank you for raising your hand, Karen." As soon as the student who was calling out raises a hand to answer a question, I will make sure to reward him or her for this positive behavior.

- When we are studying similes, I encourage students to raise their hands whenever they hear one during our read aloud. The first student to raise a hand and point out the simile gets a ticket. I do the same thing when we study other figurative and poetic devices (metaphors, alliteration, onomatopoeia, etc.).

Then, whenever we take a break during the day, students write their names on their tickets and place them in a clear plastic jar on my desk. The jar has a sign on it that says, "WEEKLY RAFFLE." Every Monday morning I shake up the jar and allow the previous week's winner to draw the winning ticket(s). There is a special beanbag chair on the rug which the winner gets to sit in whenever we go to the rug for group lessons, read alouds, class novels, discussions, etc. You might also use incentives like allowing the weekly winner to use the computer all week long while the rest of the class does their "morning work." Or, if there is a particular duty which is sought after, like being the class messenger, you could allow the winner to assume those duties. You might even consider having several weekly winners, with different prizes. I have a laminated sign on the blackboard that says, "WEEKLY WINNER." I use an erasable marker to write the winner's name on the chart for all to see.

Also, once a year, I hold "The Great Ticket Hunt." This event is used as an incentive to get the class to reach a predetermined goal. On the day of "The Great Ticket Hunt" I arrive an hour early and hide a couple of hundred tickets around the classroom. They're hidden inside the pencil sharpener, rolled up in the class maps, under the beanbag chair, etc. Once all of the students arrive for the day I announce that the hunt is on. My only rules are that no tickets are hidden on or in my desk, and that whatever they move when looking for tickets must be put back exactly as they found it. Then for the next half hour the students have a blast searching for hidden tickets. Some tickets are not found until weeks later, which always causes some laughs.

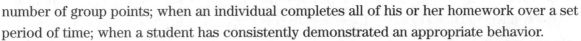

Late Pass Coupons

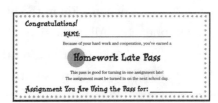

Congratulations!
NAME: _____
Because of your hard work and cooperation, you've earned a
Homework Late Pass
This pass is good for turning in one assignment late!
The assignment must be turned in on the next school day.
Assignment You Are Using the Pass for: _____

Use the coupons on page 41 as incentives for reaching short-term goals—when cooperative groups reach an assigned number of group points; when an individual completes all of his or her homework over a set period of time; when a student has consistently demonstrated an appropriate behavior.

During my first months of teaching I would hand out homework passes, which allowed students to miss an assignment without being penalized. However, I had a hard time justifying that students miss any of my assignments, believing them all to be important—otherwise I would not have assigned the work. Therefore, I use "Late Passes" which allow students to turn an assignment in one day late without being penalized. I have found them to be just as effective as a motivational tool. My students would often hold onto the late passes to use on a day when they had a particularly busy after-school schedule.

Breakfast Club

Write the names of your students down the left-hand side of a large class roster poster that you can get from a teachers' supply store. Write the dates of each of the weeks of school across the top of the grid, leaving a space after every fourth or fifth week where you'll write the words "Breakfast Club." Place a sticker under each week for students who completed all of their homework for that week satisfactorily and on time. Invite those students who have a sticker under every space for a given four- or five-week period to come to school early for a breakfast of cereal, doughnuts, juice, and milk. Ask the principal to visit during the party to offer praise to the students for their hard work.

Outdoor Activities

After all of the physical activities that students participated in over the summer break, it is hard for them to adjust to sitting in their seats during the first days of school. To aid them in making this transition, I like to take them outside to run off their pent-up energy. Here are two games that I learned from some camp counselors when I took my class on a three-day camping trip. Students loved the games so much that they wanted to play them throughout the year. I would use them as an incentive, taking them outside to play if they met a predetermined goal.

FISHY, FISHY

Take your class out to a large field. Create side boundaries and "end zones." Select four students who will be the sharks; all of the other students will be the fish. Have all of the fish stand along one end zone. Then shout out, "Fishy, fishy, come swim in my _____ ocean." Fill in the blank with words like "boy, short sleeves, brown hair, sneakers, everyone, etc." All of the fish who fall into that category have to run from one end zone to the other. The sharks can run after the fish and try to tag them. Any fish who are tagged have to stand still. They become seaweed, fixed to the bottom of the ocean. They cannot run, but they should stand there and sway, trying to tag any fish who run past them. As the game progresses it is harder for the fish to dodge the seaweed while running from the sharks. The last fish remaining is the winner. You need to adjust the size of the playing area to fit the number of players.

SHIPWRECK!

All of your student "sailors" need to gather around you in the middle of a large field for this fun-filled elimination game. You will shout out the following commands, and the sailors will need to follow the accompanying directions:

"SHIP" — The sailors will run across the field in one direction.
"WRECK" — The sailors will run across the field in the other direction.
"MAN OVERBOARD!" — Sailors pair off. One sailor crouches down, and the other stands behind him or her with a hand up to his or her forehead as if searching for someone. Any student without a partner gets "shipwrecked" and must abandon ship and sit out.
"CROW'S NEST!" — Three sailors link arms behind their backs and face outward as they turn in a circle while crowing. Any sailor not in a crow's nest must abandon ship.
"CAPTAIN'S TABLE!" — Four sailors crouch down around an imaginary table and feed their faces while making gluttonous sounds. Any sailor not at a table must abandon ship.
"WALK THE PLANK!" — Five sailors line up in a row with their right hand clasping the right shoulder of the person in front of them. They need to walk in a line while humming the funeral march. Any sailor not on the plank must abandon ship.
"CAPTAIN ON DECK!" — Everyone must stand at attention until the leader says, "At ease." If you give a command before "at ease" is said, the sailors should still remain at attention. Anyone who moves must abandon ship.

The game continues until there is only one sailor left.

Congratulations!

NAME: _____

Because of your hard work and cooperation, you've earned a

Homework Late Pass

This pass is good for turning in one assignment late!
The assignment must be turned in on the next school day.

Assignment You Are Using the Pass for: _____

Congratulations!

NAME: _____

Because of your hard work and cooperation, you've earned a

Homework Late Pass

This pass is good for turning in one assignment late!
The assignment must be turned in on the next school day.

Assignment You Are Using the Pass for: _____

Congratulations!

NAME: _____

Because of your hard work and cooperation, you've earned a

Homework Late Pass

This pass is good for turning in one assignment late!
The assignment must be turned in on the next school day.

Assignment You Are Using the Pass for: _____

Home/School Communication
For the First Week of School ... and Beyond

Dear Parents ...

On the first day of school I give my students a newsletter to take home to their parents. The newsletter contains articles about the year ahead, my teaching philosophy, my homework policy, our class rules, our first thematic unit, a list of classroom supplies which are needed, and the poem "Two Sculptors" (which can be found on page 48). I have found this to be a great way for parents (and their children) to gain a better understanding of what to expect in the coming year.

Type up your introductory article and place it onto the cover-page template on page 47. Add other articles related to your teaching style and classroom needs. Following are some suggested articles for you to use or modify. Below is some art you will find useful when putting your newsletter together. You will find more art on pages 55-56.

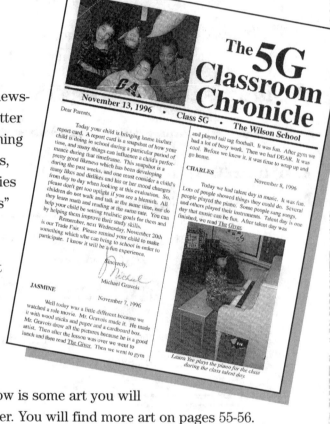

The 5G Classroom Chronicle

November 13, 1996 • Class 5G • The Wilson School

Dear Parents,

Today your child is bringing home his/her report card. A report card is a snapshot of how your child is doing in school during a particular period of time, and many things can influence a child's performance during that timeframe. This snapshot is a pretty good likeness which has been developing during the past weeks, and one must consider a child's many likes and dislikes and his or her mood changes from day to day when looking at this evaluation. So, please don't get too uptight if you see a blemish. All children do not walk and talk at the same time, nor do they learn math and reading at the same rate. You can help your child be setting realistic goals for them and by helping them improve their study skills.

Remember, next Wednesday, November 20th is our Trade Fair. Please remind your child to make something which s/he can bring to school in order to participate. I know it will be a fun experience.

Sincerely,
Michael Gravois

JASMINE   November 7, 1996

Well today was a little different because we watched a role movie. Mr. Gravois made it. He made it with wood sticks and paper and a cardboard box. Mr. Gravois drew all the pictures because he is a good artist. Then after the lesson was over we went to lunch and then read The Giver. Then we went to gym

and played tail tag football. It was fun. After gym we had a lot of busy work. Then we had DEAR. It was cool. Before we knew it, it was time to wrap up and go home.

CHARLES

Today we had talent day in music. It was fun. Lots of people showed things they could do. Several people played the piano. Some could do. And others played their instruments. People sang songs, day that music can be fun. Talent day is one finished, we read The Giver.

Laura Yee plays the piano for the class during the class talent day.

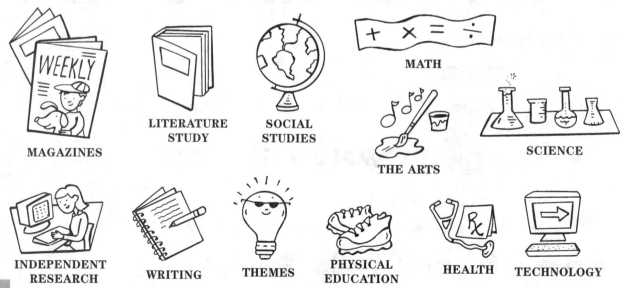

MAGAZINES

LITERATURE STUDY

SOCIAL STUDIES

MATH

THE ARTS

SCIENCE

INDEPENDENT RESEARCH

WRITING

THEMES

PHYSICAL EDUCATION

HEALTH

TECHNOLOGY

Introductory Article

Dear Parents,

This is a very special time in your child's life. He or she will be learning many new things this year—academic skills, organizational skills, social skills, self-confidence, and responsibility. In fact, the year your child spends in fifth grade will be one of the most important and valuable years in his or her development, readying him or her for the less structured years ahead in intermediate school.

You play a major role in helping your child reach the maximum of his or her potential. Research in the area of child development points out that most of a child's intellectual development takes place outside the formal classroom. This means that children spend a great deal of time with their first and most important teachers—their parents. Indeed, as parents, your involvement in your child's learning experiences will have much to do with how well your child succeeds in school and in later life. By working together, I believe we can all help your child become the best person possible—socially, emotionally, and scholastically.

I have prepared this newsletter to introduce myself, to share some of my philosophies on teaching, and to give you and your child some ideas as to what to expect over the course of the next year.

If you have any questions or concerns throughout the year, please do not hesitate to contact me. Unless it is an emergency, I would appreciate a note or phone call requesting a meeting time so that I will be able to give you and your child my undivided attention.

In order to keep you informed of your child's progress, I will be sending home a weekly newsletter announcing upcoming projects, reporting on the previous week's activities, and requesting special needs our class might have. A weekly evaluation of your child's work will accompany the newsletter.

I'm looking forward to working with you this year as we help your child experience all the joys of learning. I stand ready to assist you in any way I can, so please feel free to get in touch with me at any time. Your participation and encouragement will be major contributions to your child's success this year!

Sincerely,

My Teaching Philosophy

Everyone wants to know that there is a purpose for doing anything requiring an effort—and school certainly does require effort. It is for this reason that I employ a theme-based approach to my teaching methods as much as possible. It helps children understand the purpose for learning.

A theme-based approach to teaching organizes materials and activities around a central topic, providing a natural link between the different areas of the curriculum. By surrounding the class in the theme, links are established between the content areas, and meaning is generated.

By immersing the students in a thematic study unit, they will discover that the skills they are learning have applications beyond just getting answers right on a test. They will become intent on finding out the answers to the questions they are asking to satisfy their own curiosity, rather than just because they were told, "Because it's important to learn this."

article continued on following page

Each theme will be announced in my weekly newsletter. Please feel free to share any theme-related books from home which may add variety to our classroom library. Or perhaps you may have an expertise in a related area and would like to come into the classroom to present material on the subject. I highly encourage home/school interactions.

I also believe in stressing all of the language arts—reading, writing, speaking, and listening—as well as the visual arts. The development of any of these skills increases the child's proficiency in each of the other areas.

It is my goal to make your child an active seeker of knowledge, rather than just a passive recipient, and I will use each of the subject areas as the tools for learning. I will use weekly, bi-weekly, or monthly themes to involve my students in constructing meaning, discovering relationships, solving problems, and developing skills through meaningful practice.

Homework Policy

As an incentive for students to complete all of their homework on time, I hold a monthly "Breakfast Club" party. Any student who has completed all of his or her homework on time in a given month will be invited to a breakfast before school.

I expect all homework assignments to be handed in on time. Any missed assignments during a given week will be listed each Friday on my weekly evaluation of your child's progress. Students will have until Monday, or the next school day, to complete any missed assignments for that week. However, the grade for that assignment will be lowered by one letter grade. Failure to turn in the work by the next school day will result in a zero for that assignment.

Class Rules

At the beginning of each year I establish a few simple rules which I expect each student in my class to obey. My rules are based on a respect for others and for the property of others. Please feel free to visit our classroom after school one day during the coming week to look over these rules.

Also hanging in our class, I have a list of "Rewards and Consequences" which we discussed as a class. In brief, if a rule is broken, students will first be given a verbal warning; with a second warning they will need to write a two-paragraph apology describing what they did and why that behavior cannot be allowed (signed by parent); with a third warning they will have to write the apology, I will call the parents, and the student will have to arrive at school 15 minutes early before the next school day.

In The News

In order to initiate interest in current events, we will discuss a newspaper or magazine article each day. I have given each student an "In The News" calendar detailing the date they are to bring in an article which interests them. They can use the "In The News" outline to aid them in organizing information from their article for their short presentation.

Perhaps they were required to do something similar to this in an earlier grade and therefore feel comfortable selecting an arti-cle on their own. If not, you may consider helping them choose an article the first time they are scheduled to present one.

First-Week Phone Calls

On the first day of school I tell my students that their parents should expect a phone call from me sometime over the course of the next three days. I then call each child's parent(s) to introduce myself, find out what their expectations are for the year ahead, and to find out if there are any particular areas on which they would like to see me focus regarding their child's education. The information I collect is not only invaluable in helping me understand my students as quickly as possible, but it delights the parents to know that I am taking an active interest in their child. The parental response to my phone calls is always incredibly positive, and it starts the year off on the right note.

Weekly Evaluations

During my planning period every Friday I fill out a weekly evaluation for each student listing any homework missed during the week, test scores from the week, classroom behavior, and other comments. See the form on page 49. Students are responsible for having their parents sign the form and for returning it on Monday morning. This assures me that the parents are aware of their child's weekly progress. It also allows me the opportunity to respond individually to each parent, if needed, without having to make evening phone calls. Be sure to offer praise as well as criticism on these forms, so students know that good work is rewarded.

Homework Checklist

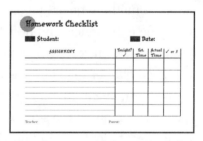

Occasionally you will have a student who has an extremely difficult time completing homework. Phone calls to parents and reprimands don't always seem to work. Sometimes the student needs a little extra attention in order to learn how to budget time and focus on the task at hand.

Spend an extra five or ten minutes after school with this student detailing the day's homework using the homework checklist on page 49. List each assignment and the estimated amount of time you and the student feel it should take to complete each assignment. Also list any long-term assignments on the form. Place a check mark in the first column next to any assignment that must be completed that night. Sign your name at the bottom. These individual sessions will give both you and the student better insight into his or her work habits.

When each assignment is complete, the student should write the actual amount of time it took. He or she should also put a check mark next to all of the assignments worked on, and an "X" next to any not worked on. An "X" can only be next to long-term assignments that are not due the next day. When the student finishes the homework, parents should review the checklist and make sure the required work is completed. They should sign the bottom of the form to alert the teacher that they checked the homework. (Let the parents know that they should not check the homework for content, only for completion. You will check the content.) The student should turn the form in along with the completed assignments. If you, the student, and the parents work together, you can help the child develop the necessary skills to be able to self-monitor in the future. After one successful month, tell the student that you will suspend the checklist procedure. If the child lapses again, reinstitute this procedure.

The Classroom Chronicle

A weekly class newsletter is a powerful tool that can be used to foster home/school communication. However, creating one seems like it would be an overwhelming burden for you to coordinate. If the task is shared with students you can produce a weekly newsletter quickly and easily. This also allows you to publish students' writing on a regular basis.

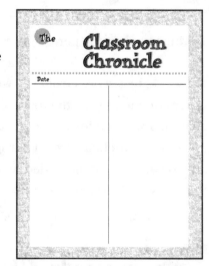

At the beginning of the year buy a composition notebook and create a cover for it entitled "The Classroom Chronicle." Each night send the notebook home with a different student who will write two or three complete paragraphs about something he or she did that day, what was learned from the experience, and how he or she felt about the day's activities. The next day that student will type the information into the computer under a pre-designed banner reading "The Classroom Chronicle." The student should include the date and his or her name at the top of the article. By the end of the week five different students will have written about the school day and added the article to the computer. (If no computers are available, students should neatly rewrite the information onto a sheet of paper.)

At the end of the week, write a brief article that describes your thoughts about the past week, information about upcoming events and thematic units, requests for parent volunteers, etc. Add the five articles that the students wrote, include some related clip art, copy the newsletters, and send them home to the parents. If your school has a digital camera, consider taking snapshots of your students each week to add to the newsletter. Parents will appreciate being kept well informed and they will enjoy reading about students' experiences.

The Classroom Chronicle

Date _____

Two Sculptors

I dreamed I saw a studio
And watched two sculptors there.
The clay they used was a child's mind
And they fashioned it with care.

One was a teacher—the tools he used
Were books, music, and art.
The other, a parent, worked with a guiding hand,
And a gentle, loving heart.

Day after day, the teacher toiled with a touch
That was careful, deft, and sure,
While the parent labored by his side
And polished and smoothed it o'er.

And when at last, their task was done,
They were proud of what they had wrought.
For the things they had molded into the child
Could neither be sold nor bought.

And each agreed they would have failed
If either had worked alone.
For behind the parent stood the school
And behind the teacher, the home.

Anonymous

Weekly Evaluation

This is what we did this week:
Reading
Math Language

■ **Name:** _____

■ **Date:** _____

Homework/Classwork missed for the week:

_____

_____

_____

(All missed work due on Monday, or on the next day of school.)

Behavior for the week: ❑ Satisfactory   ❑ Unsatisfactory

Comments & Test Grades:

_____

_____

_____

Parent Signature:

Homework Checklist

■ **Student:** _____

■ **Date:** _____

ASSIGNMENT	Tonight? ✓	Est. Time	Actual Time	✓ or ✗

Teacher: Parent:

Back-To-School Night

Parent/Teacher Conferences

Wanted: Parent Volunteers

Every teacher should rely on parent volunteers to help chaperone field trips, aid in classroom activities, or give presentations on subjects in which they are knowledgeable. When the parents arrive on Back-to-School Night, include the "Wanted: Parent Volunteers" sheet on page 52 as part of their packet. Ask them to fill it out and to have their child bring it to you the next day.

About My Child

Parental input is an important ingredient in fully understanding the needs of your students and the expectations that parents have of their child and of the year ahead. Include the "About My Child" assignment as part of the Back-to-School Night packet, and ask parents to return it to you as soon as possible. This information will help you to better understand your students and their parents.

Parent-Teacher Conferences Confirmation Sheets

Before parents arrive for Back-to-School Night, I prepare a "Parent-Teacher Conference Sign-up Sheet." On it, I have a column with the heading TIME, and list preselected conference times. The column next to it has the heading NAME. As parents enter your classroom on Back-to-School Night, I ask them to write their names next to a time that is convenient for them to meet with me. Allowing parents to select times that are convenient for them saves you the trouble of trying to coordinate the schedule. However, you will have to arrange times to meet with parents who didn't attend Back-to-School Night or for those parents who are unable to attend any of the scheduled times. A couple of days before the conferences send a confirmation sheet home with each child verifying the times the parents had selected (see page 53).

Student Information Form

Be prepared for the parent-teacher conference by spending a few minutes filling out a "Student Information Form" on page 54 for each student. Use the information you gathered from your first-week phone calls (see page 45) and from the "About My Child" activity (see the related section on page 50) to fill in the column entitled "Information Shared By Parents." A week or two before the conferences, ask students to write a few paragraphs that answer the following questions, and use this information to fill in the column entitled "Information Shared by Student."

- ◼ What do you feel your academic strengths are?
- ◼ In which areas do you feel you need to improve most?
- ◼ How do you think you could improve in these areas?
- ◼ What have you enjoyed most about school so far this year?
- ◼ What did you enjoy least?
- ◼ What are you most proud of this school year?
- ◼ Is there anything in particular that you want me to discuss with your parents during the parent/teacher conference?

Fill in the third column entitled "Information Shared by Teacher" based on your experiences with each student. Point out the child's strengths, weaknesses, accomplishments, and your observations. When parents arrive for the conference, review this sheet with them. Explain how you are going to fulfill their expectations of the coming school year; share your observations about the parental and student input; and discuss the information you have developed based on your experiences with their child. Having the information readily available ensures that you don't overlook anything important and presents you as a prepared and concerned teacher. It also helps calm any nerves you might have about the conferences because you know exactly what you want to say about each child.

STUDENT INFORMATION FORM

Student's Name: Jane Doe
Teacher: Michael Bronois
Participants: Mr. Joe Doe
Ms. Sally Doe

Date: 11/5
Time: 2:00 - 2:20

INFORMATION SHARED BY PARENTS	INFORMATION SHARED BY STUDENT	INFORMATION SHARED BY TEACHER
• very imaginative and creative	• enjoys being in 5th grade	• Jane is always smiling and laughing
• feels she can't do what others can do	• enjoys experiments	• she has one of the kindest hearts in the class — very nurturing;
• can't really recall comprehension	• loved Fairview Lakes camping trip	a pleasure to see this in her
• gets anxious and frustrated preparing an assignment	• likes using the computers	• while speed is an issue, she seems to grasp concepts
• spelling while pre-writing is a problem	• didn't like Tuck Everlasting	• her major hurdle is in writing
• HW takes a long time	• hates music class	
	• really, really hates HW	
	• needs to work on spelling	

Comments: Get back to John and Sally with a copy of the Homework Checklist form; hopefully this will help Jane focus on completing her HW more quickly.

WANTED: Parent Volunteers!

Dear Parents,

Throughout the year I like to supplement my teaching with guest speakers who are knowledgeable in areas of the curriculum we are studying. I also rely on parent volunteers to help chaperone field trips and aid in classroom activities. Please complete this form and return it to me as soon as possible. Thanks for your help in making this a fulfilling and exciting school year.

Sincerely,

Parent(s): _____   Child: _____

Address: _____   Phone: _____

Occupation(s) _____   Hobbies: _____

Other areas of expertise: _____

I would be happy to: ❏ Go on field trips   ❏ Help with classroom activities   ❏ Be a guest speaker
    ❏ Supply materials for the classroom   ❏ Make phone calls   ❏ Other_____

Comments: _____

_____

_____

About My Child

Dear Parents,

I enjoyed telling you about your child's life at school. So that I may get to know you and your child better, I would like for you to tell me a little about your child's life at home. Please answer the following questions (use the back of this paper if necessary), and return it to me as soon as possible. Your input is appreciated and invaluable

Sincerely,

- Describe your child as a person.
- What are your expectations for your child's school year?
- What does your child say about school at home?
- What are your child's interests and strengths?
- In what areas do you think your child needs to improve?
- You may also include any other information which you feel may be valuable for me to know.

Parent(s): _____   Child: _____

_____

_____

_____

Confirmation Sheet

Dear _____,

    I am looking forward to meeting with you to discuss _____ progress. I have scheduled our conference time on _____ at _____. Please indicate whether or not this time is convenient for you and return this confirmation sheet to me.

                                              Sincerely,

____ The appointment is satisfactory.

____ I am unable to meet with you at the time you suggest. Please call me to arrange a different time.

Confirmation Sheet

Dear _____,

    I am looking forward to meeting with you to discuss _____ progress. I have scheduled our conference time on _____ at _____. Please indicate whether or not this time is convenient for you and return this confirmation sheet to me.

                                              Sincerely,

____ The appointment is satisfactory.

____ I am unable to meet with you at the time you suggest. Please call me to arrange a different time.

Confirmation Sheet

Dear _____,

    I am looking forward to meeting with you to discuss _____ progress. I have scheduled our conference time on _____ at _____. Please indicate whether or not this time is convenient for you and return this confirmation sheet to me.

                                              Sincerely,

____ The appointment is satisfactory.

____ I am unable to meet with you at the time you suggest. Please call me to arrange a different time.

STUDENT INFORMATION FORM

Student's Name: _____

Teacher: _____

Participants: _____

Date: _____

Time: _____

INFORMATION SHARED BY STUDENT

_____

_____

_____

_____

_____

_____

_____

_____

_____

_____

INFORMATION SHARED BY TEACHER

_____

_____

_____

_____

_____

_____

_____

_____

_____

_____

INFORMATION SHARED BY PARENTS

_____

_____

_____

_____

_____

_____

_____

_____

_____

_____

Comments: _____

_____

_____

WELCOME TO SCHOOL